American Humane®

Protecting
Children & Animals
Since 1877

American Humane Pet   Care Library

Cats

How
to
Choose
and
Care
for
a Cat

Laura S. Jeffrey

Enslow Publishers, Inc.

40 Industrial Road   PO Box 38
Box 398   Aldershot
Berkeley Heights, NJ 07922 Hants GU12 6BP
USA   UK

http://www.enslow.com

American Humane ®

Protecting
Children & Animals
Since 1877

The American Humane Association is dedicated to preventing the cruelty, abuse, neglect, and exploitation of children and animals. To learn how you can support the vision of a nation where no child or animal will ever be a victim of willful abuse or neglect, visit www.americanhumane.org, phone (303) 792-9900, or write American Humane at 63 Inverness Drive East, Englewood, Colorado, 80112-5117.

Library of Congress Cataloging-in-Publication Data

Jeffrey, Laura S.
    Cats: how to choose and care for a cat / Laura S. Jeffrey.
        p. cm. — (American humane pet care library)
    Summary: Provides information on cats as pets, including how to choose among different
        breeds, find a cat to buy or adopt, and how to feed and keep a cat healthy.
    Includes bibliographical references and index.
    ISBN 0-7660-2516-0
    1. Cats—Juvenile literature. [1. Cats 2. Pets] I. Title.
    SF445.7.J456 2004
    636.8—dc22

                                    2003022967

Printed in the United States of America

10 9 8 7 6 5 4 3 2

To Our Readers: We have done our best to make sure all Internet Addresses in this book were active and appropriate when we went to press. However, the author and the publisher have no control over and assume no liability for the material available on those Internet sites or on other Web sites they may link to. Any comments or suggestions can be sent by e-mail to comments@enslow.com or to the address on the back cover.

Every effort has been made to locate all copyright holders of material used in this book. If any errors or omissions have occurred, corrections will be made in future editions of this book.

Photo Credits: © 1996–2004 ArtToday, Inc., pp. 7 (right), 9, 11 (right), 13, 16, 17, 20, 22, 23 (top), 24, 26 (top), 27 (right), 31, 34, 35, 37; John Bavaro, pp. 42, 43; Corel Corporation, pp. 10, 18, 21, 26 (bottom); courtesy of Pam Deisher, p. 45; EyeWire, pp. 4, 6, 14, 25, 36; Hemera Technologies, Inc. 1997–2000, pp. 15 (right), 23 (bottom), 28 (bottom), 29; Painet, Inc., p. 38; PhotoDisc, Inc., pp. 1, 3, 5 (right), 8, 28 (top), 30, 33 (right), 41 (right); © 2002 PIXTAL, pp. 5 (left), 7 (left), 11 (left), 12, 15 (left), 27 (left), 32, 33 (left), 39, 40, 41 (left).

Cover Illustration: Corel Corporation (Horse); PhotoDisc, Inc. (Gerbil, Dog, Fish, Cat, Bird).

Contents

Cats are
beautiful,
smart, and
playful.

Great Pets

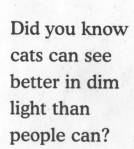

 Cats are great pets. They are beautiful, smart, and playful. They are fun to watch as they pounce on toys, swat at balls, and stretch after a long nap.. Cats enjoy people as well as other cats, but they also like to be by themselves. They are happy to be on their own. Cats are easy to care for, and they are easy to love. For all of these reasons, cats are popular pets. Millions of Americans have at least one cat in their home.

This book will help you choose the right cat for you. It will tell you what to feed your new pet and how to make it feel comfortable and safe. You will learn how to keep your cat healthy and happy.

Did you know cats can see better in dim light than people can?

There are many different breeds of cats all over the world.

The History of Cats

 Long, long ago, cats were wild animals. But cats have been household pets for about four thousand years. The ancient Egyptians were the first to make cats household pets. They used cats to protect food supplies from rats and other pests. The ancient Egyptians thought of cats as gods and goddesses. They had laws against killing cats. People who killed cats could be put to death.

Ancient Egyptians drew pictures of cats on walls. They were the first to have cats as pets.

By the 1700s, people all over the world had cats as pets. Cats came to America with the Pilgrims. Cats were used on the *Mayflower* and other ships to hunt rats. Cats became more than just workers for people. They became friends.

Today, there are millions of cats in the world. There are about thirty-five different breeds. Cats can also be mixtures of different breeds. Some cats are solid colored. Others have color patterns such as stripes, spots, or patches. Cats may have short hair or long hair, smooth coats or even curly coats. Some cats have a long, fluffy tail while others have a short, stubby tail. Some cats have ears that fold down, while others have ears that stand up.

Fast Fact

Today, there are many cultures that believe cats bring good fortune.

For purebred cats, the American shorthair is a popular cat breed. This breed is known for its beauty and gentle nature. American shorthairs get along well with children and dogs. They come in about eighty different colors and patterns. The most common American shorthair is silver with black markings.

Siamese cats come from Thailand, which was once called Siam. Siamese cats have short, light-colored coats. They have darker blue, brown, lilac, lynx, or red markings on their legs, tail, ears, and face. Siamese cats like to sit in their owner's lap. Some people think the purring of a Siamese cat sounds like singing.

Siamese cats are just one type of breed.

Cats can live for an average of ten to fifteen years. With proper care, they will give their owners love and friendship for many years.

Before deciding
which cat you
would like, you
have to think
about whether
you want a
kitten or a cat.

3

The Right Cat for You

 What kind of cat is best for you? First, you should decide if you want a cat or a kitten. Kittens are adorable. A kitten is a friend and playmate, not a toy. If you have a younger brother or sister, you probably should get a cat instead of a kitten. Cats can be playful and silly, too.

Another decision is what breed of cat to get. Some cat breeds are better for children and families. You can learn about the different breeds of cats through the Internet or library books.

Cats can use sound, body signals, and scents as ways to communicate.

If the adults in your house agree, you may want to adopt two cats instead of just one. Most cats enjoy company. They also like to have fun late at night. Having two cats means there will always be a playmate for the other one.

Pet Pointer

Cats should never go outside by themselves. They can get hurt by cars, dogs, bad people, or wild animals.

Where Will You Get Your New Pet?

Your first stop should be your local animal shelter. There, you will find many healthy, adorable, and loving cats and kittens in need of a home. Most of the cats and kittens in the shelter will probably be mixed breeds.

Workers at the shelter have gotten to know these animals. They will help match you with the right pet for your family. Also, adopting a pet is the best way to help animals.

If you want a certain type of cat that is not currently available at the shelter, ask shelter workers about a breed-placement group. This is a group of concerned people who take in unwanted cats and find homes for them.

Cats are just as playful as kittens.

You can also buy a cat or kitten from a breeder. However, breeders may charge a lot of money.

The American Humane Association says people should not get a cat from a pet store. Pet stores are not as concerned about matching people with a pet that will fit well into their lifestyle.

Be sure to give your new pet time to get to know you and its new home.

Taking Care of Your Cat

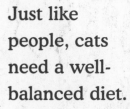

4

You probably cannot wait to spend time holding and playing with your new cat. But you need to give it plenty of time to get to know its new home. You also need to give it time to get to know you. When you first bring your cat home, keep it in one room. The cat will feel more secure if it learns its way around one room at a time. Let the cat slowly explore its new home. Slowly and quietly let it meet other family members and household pets. In time, cats adapt happily to any house or apartment. They never need to go

Just like people, cats need a well-balanced diet.

outside, where cars, diseases, other cats, dogs, and bad people can harm them.

Eating

Always have a bowl of fresh, cool drinking water for your cat. Do not give your cat milk because it may cause diarrhea. Feed your cat a high-quality, brand-name food made for cats. The three main types are dry, soft-moist, and canned. Always feed your cat in the same place and at the same time. Do not touch or bother your cat while it is eating.

Do not feed your cat human food because it may not have the right kinds of nutrients your pet needs. Also, cats should never be fed bones or raw fish.

Always have a bowl of water out for your cat.

Kittens should stay with their mothers until they are at least eight weeks old so they can drink their mother's milk. If you adopt a kitten younger than this, ask a veterinarian how to feed it.

Sleeping

Cats take plenty of long naps. They like to sleep in a padded, shallow box or basket. They may also end up choosing their own resting place, such as your bed or a sunny windowsill. Cats may sleep as much as eighteen hours a day.

Using the Litter Box

The best toilet for your cat is a plastic litter pan. Cover the bottom of the pan with about two inches of litter. Put the pan someplace where your cat will not be bothered or annoyed by other pets or household activity. Make sure the pan is far away from the cat's food and water bowls.

Cats use a litter box. Some are pans with no tops. Others, like this one, are enclosed.

Cats like to
sleep a lot!
They like cozy
places like
their own bed,
but they may
find their own
special place
to sleep.

Your cat will naturally want to use the pan, so you should not have to worry about training it. Just make sure your cat knows where the pan is. In a two-story house, you might need one pan upstairs and another one downstairs. A very young kitten may need a few litter pans at first.

Keep the litter pan clean. Otherwise, your cat may decide to use the corner of a room instead. Scoop out the waste at least once a day. Change the litter and wash the box with a mild soap every few weeks or as often as needed.

Identification

Buy your cat a collar that has an elastic insert. If your cat gets caught on something, the elastic in the collar will expand so the cat can free itself without getting hurt.

On the collar, place an identification (ID) tag with your family's name, address, and phone number on it. Even a house cat might slip through an open door or window and become lost. An identification tag lets neighbors or animal shelter workers return your pet to you. Also, ask the adults you live with to find out if you need a city or county license for your cat.

In case your cat gets lost, a tag on a collar has the contact information to get your cat returned to you.

A microchip is a very small computer chip. More and more people are having vets put microchip IDs into their cats. This is a safe and effective way to have a permanent ID for your cat. However, some people who find cats do not know that they may have a microchip. So it is a good idea to have an identification tag on your pet's collar at all times. That way, you are helping your pet find its way home if it ever becomes lost.

Have information
ready about your
cat in case there
is an emergency.

In case your pet gets outside accidentally and becomes lost, or in case of an emergency such as a fire or flood, have information about your pet ready to share. This includes a recent photo, vaccination records, vet information, and names and phone numbers to contact.

Pet Pointer

Be sure your cat is always wearing a tag and collar with its name and your family's address on it. The best way is to have your cat micro-chipped to make sure it is returned home safely if it becomes lost.

Grooming

You will not need to bathe your pet because cats clean themselves with their very rough tongue.

But some cats do enjoy baths. If you give your cat a bath, use warm water and mild soap. Do not use a shampoo used for dogs because it could harm your cat. Let your cat dry off in a warm place.

Cats swallow pieces of hair as they clean themselves.

Even though you will not have to bathe your cat often, you should regularly brush its coat. Brushing helps prevent hair balls. When cats lick their coats to clean themselves, they swallow pieces of hair. The hair forms a ball in the cat's stomach.

Fast Fact

Milk can upset your cat's stomach.

Sometimes, cats throw up hair balls. Regular combing can help prevent hair balls from forming. Longhaired cats should be combed daily with a steel comb. A brush works well on shorthaired cats.

You can also buy a paste to feed your cat as a treat. The paste will help the cat pass the hair through its body instead of throwing it up as a hair ball.

Sometimes your cat might need a bath with warm water and mild soap.

Praising and talking to your cat will make your cat more loving.

Praising

Most cats love attention. Make sure you talk to your pet. Praise or say good things to your cat when it is good, and include it in your day-to-day activities, when possible. Remember that your gentle words and behavior will make your cat even more loving.

Some kittens might be too young to adopt. Ask your local animal shelter if a kitten is ready to be adopted. Small kittens need to be fed with a bottle.

5

Healthy and Happy

A veterinarian, often called a vet, is a doctor who takes care of sick and hurt animals. A vet also makes sure animals stay healthy. Soon after you bring your cat home, make an appointment with your vet. The vet will examine your cat and make sure it is healthy. The vet also will schedule the shots your new pet needs to protect it from diseases. One of these diseases is rabies. If a cat with rabies bites or scratches you, then you could get rabies, too.

Other health concerns for cats are intestinal parasites and heartworm. Also, cats are more

Be sure to take your pet to a vet for checkups.

27

Spaying or neutering your cat is helpful. Behavioral problems will lessen, and your cat may even become more loving.

likely than dogs to catch diseases that cause breathing trouble.

Ask your veterinarian how you can tell when your cat is sick. Also ask about how to get help if there is an emergency after the vet's regular office hours. That way, you will know when and how to get help for your pet.

For example, cats have a third eyelid, called the nictitating membrane. This third eyelid sometimes can be seen when a cat gets sick. Also, cats that are sick may stop using their litter box. They go to the bathroom in other areas of the house.

Spaying and Neutering

The vet will want to talk to you and the adults you live with about getting your cat spayed, if it is a female, or neutered, if it is a male. To spay or neuter is to operate on an animal so it cannot reproduce. Spaying and neutering prevent overpopulation.

Fast Fact

Cats clean themselves with their very rough tongues.

Every year, millions of lovable cats and kittens must be euthanized, or put to death, in animal shelters because there are no homes for them. If your cat is eight weeks or older, it is old enough to be spayed or neutered. Most animals in local shelters are spayed or neutered before they are put up for adoption.

There are not enough homes for all the cats alive today, so do not let your cat have kittens.

Spaying and neutering are safe operations. Also, the operation may be helpful to your cat. Neutered males lose their urge to roam and fight with other cats. Cats are less likely to spray where they should not. They usually become calmer and more loving.

Playing

To make sure your cat stays healthy, play with your cat. Playing is how cats get their exercise. You can buy toys for your cat at a pet supply store, or you can use objects around the house. Cats love things that they can chase, pull, or swat. They like small, round objects such as Ping-Pong balls and golf balls. They enjoy playing with wadded-up paper and in boxes. Cats also like to climb into paper bags. Remember that plastic bags can be dangerous for cats, just as they are dangerous for humans.

Cats like to play. Give them toys that are safe for them, like this ball.

31

Kittens and cats can be trained, but be patient with them!

6

Preventing Problems

Training

Cats are sensitive and smart. Because of these traits, they can be trained. Your pet can learn to come when its name is called. It can also learn to stop doing something when you say "no." Some cats can perform tricks. They can also be trained to use the toilet instead of a litter box.

But cats are not as easy to train as dogs are. If you try to train your cat, remain calm and keep doing the same thing. Like dogs, cats respond to food rewards and attention.

Some household plants are poisonous to cats. Be sure plants are kept away from where a cat can get to them. You can grow special grasses just for your cat.

They will not change their behavior if you punish them, so you should never hit a cat.

Scratching

Scratching is one cat behavior that humans find annoying. But for cats, scratching is normal and necessary behavior. You need to have a place where your cat can scratch, or it will find its own place. Your pet could tear up carpeting or furniture with its claws.

To prevent problems, get your cat a scratching post. You can buy one at a pet supply store. Or you can make one with a special rope called sisal. Some cats like horizontal (across) scratching surfaces. Others

Cats like to scratch. Buying your pet a special scratching post will save your curtains and furniture.

prefer vertical (up-and-down) ones. Avoid scratching posts with carpeting because this might confuse cats. They may think it is OK to scratch any carpeting in the house.

Use thick plastic to cover places in the house that you want to protect from scratching. Your cat will learn to avoid these places. Then, you can safely remove the plastic.

Some veterinarians de-claw cats to prevent them from scratching. Many animal experts say that de-clawing is cruel. Instead, trim your cat's nails to protect you and your furniture from scratches. A vet can show you how to give your cat a proper manicure. If you cut the nails too short, you could hit a bundle of nerves called the quick.

Trim your cat's nails to protect you from scratches.

Cats are very curious and can easily get into trouble. Place things like plants and fish bowls out of their reach.

Keeping Out of Trouble

Cats are very curious, but their curiosity can get them into trouble. The best solution is to remove items that cats will want to check out. Keep food off the kitchen counter. Place houseplants out of your cat's reach. Make sure items such as household cleaners, medicine, makeup, and needles and thread are safely put away.

Also, remember to close the door of the clothes dryer. Cats love warm places. If the dryer door is open, a cat may climb inside after a load of clothes has been removed. But your pet may be overlooked when the next load of clothes is thrown in.

Cats like spending time inside in high places where they can keep an eye on people and other household pets. Keep your windowsills and the tops of tall furniture empty so your cat will have a safe place to hang out.

Cats love to hide and play.

37

Keep windowsills empty so your cat can enjoy the outside view.

Be aware that cats can climb to the highest and most dangerous shelf in the house.

Cats also can pull open cabinet drawers unless the drawers are secured in some way. Also, many cats can squeeze through small openings in windows and doors. Be sure that window screens are secure, especially the windows on high floors.

Allergies

Sometimes, people bring a cat home and then discover they are allergic to it. Actually, they are allergic to the cat's dander. Dander is the tiny flakes of dried skin or hair on a cat's skin. People who are allergic to cats sneeze or get itchy eyes and skin rashes when they get near cats.

You can buy sprays for a cat's coat to lessen the amount of dander. You can also take medicine to prevent allergic reactions.

Pet Pointer

Keeping the house vacuumed and brushing your cat daily are two ways to make life easier for people allergic to cats.

Have fun
playing and
loving your
pet for
many years.

7

You and Your New Cat

After you bring a cat into your home, you will be happy to spend time with it there.

Remember that cats can live to be over twenty years old. Keep loving and learning more about your pet, and you and your cat will spend many happy years together.

You can find more information about cats at a library or on the Internet. (Ask an adult to help you.)

Life Cycle

2.

After several months, a cat's eyes will change to their permanent color. Cats are fully grown by the time they are one year old.

1. A newborn kitten weighs about 4 ounces and is three inches long. It has no teeth and its eyes are closed. After several days a kitten will open its eyes. All kittens' eyes are blue.

# of a Cat

3. Cats enjoy playing for most of their lives. With proper care, they can live ten to fifteen years.

Words to Know

breed—To control when an animal reproduces; a group of animals with similar features.

dander—Tiny bits from skin or hair that may cause allergies.

hair ball—A rounded mass of hair that forms in an animal's stomach because the animal licks itself.

litter—Small pieces of clay used in a box for animal droppings.

microchip—A very small computer chip put inside an animal as an identification tag.

mixed breed—Having features from more than one breed of animal.

neuter—To perform an operation so a male animal cannot reproduce.

purebred—Belonging to a breed with the same features through many generations of animals.

quick—A very sensitive area underneath a nail.

sisal—A strong fiber used to make rope and other items.

spay—To perform an operation so a female animal cannot reproduce.

veterinarian—A doctor who takes care of animals instead of people.

Learn More About Cats

Books

Bishop, Amanda, and Bobbie Kalman. *What is a Cat?* New York: Crabtree Publishing Co., 2003.

Crisp, Marty. *Everything Cat: What Kids Really Want to Know About Cats.* Chanhassen, Minn.: NorthWord Press, 2003

Hinds, Kathryn. *Cats.* New York: Benchmark Books, 1999.

Internet Addresses

Bow Wow Meow

<http://www.bowwow.com.au/>
Need a name for your new pet? Check out this Web site.

Just For Kids: Cats

<http://www.americanhumane.org/kids/cats.htm>
Learn more about cats from this site by the American Humane Association.

Index

A

adoption, 12, 13, 17, 26, 30

allergies, 39

American Humane Association, 13

animal shelter, 12, 13, 20, 26, 30

B

balls, 31

behavioral problems, 28

breathing trouble, 28

breeders, 13

breed-placement group, 13

breeds, 6, 8, 9, 11, 12

  American Shorthair, 9

  Siamese, 9

C

care, 5, 43

  bathing, 22, 23, 24

  brushing, 23, 39

  clipping claws, 35

collar, 19, 20, 22

curiosity, 36

D

dander, 39

de-claw, 35

diet, 15, 16, 26

  and milk, 16, 17, 23

  cat food, 16

  drinking water, 16

  human food, 16

E

Egyptians, 7

emergency, 21, 22, 28

euthanized, 30

exercise, 31

G

grooming, 22, 29

H

health concerns, 27

  diarrhea, 16

  hair balls, 23, 24

  heartworms, 27

  intestinal parasites, 27

  poisonous plants, 33

  rabies, 27

horizontal scratching, 34

household pets, 7, 15

hunting, 8

47

I

identification, 19, 20

K

kittens, 10, 11, 12, 13, 17, 19, 26, 30, 32, 42

L

license, 20
light, 5
litter box, 17, 19, 29, 33
   changing and cleaning, 19

M

Mayflower, 8
microchip, 20, 22
mixed breeds, 12

N

napping, 5, 17

neutering, 28, 29, 30
nictitating membrane, 29

O

outside, 12, 16
overpopulation, 29

P

pet store, 13
Pilgrims, 8
playing, 31, 43
pounce, 5
praising, 25
purebred, 9

S

safety, 36-38
scratching, 34, 35
scratching post, 34, 35
sense of smell, 11
shampoo, 22

sisal rope, 34
sleeping, 17, 18
spaying, 28, 29, 30
steel comb, 24

T

talking to, 25
Thailand, 9
third eyelid, 29
toys, 5, 31
training, 19, 32, 33
tricks, 33

V

vaccination, 22, 27
vertical scratching, 35
veterinarian, 17, 20, 22, 27, 28, 29, 35

W

wild, 7